Sailing the Bright Stream

Sailing the Bright Stream

New & Selected Poems

by

David T. Manning

Press 53
Winston-Salem

Press 53, LLC
PO Box 30314
Winston-Salem, NC 27130

First Edition

Cover design by Claire V. Foxx

Cover art, "Landscape with Islands in Water,"
Copyright © 2019 by Elinalee,
licensed through iStock

Author photo by Ellen Giamportone

"Time of White Ice," Copyright 2000, *Christian Century*,
reprinted with permission from the December 20-27,
2000, issue of the *Christian Century*

Library of Congress Control Number
2020943767

Printed on acid-free paper
ISBN 978-1-950413-25-6

to Doris McKeand Manning
for her unending love and patience
with a poet husband over the years

The author would like to thank the following for their publication of individual poems, sometimes in slightly different versions or with different titles:

32 Poems Magazine: "Mirella"
Asheville Poetry Review: "The Ancient Chorister"
Bay Leaves (The Poetry Council of North Carolina):
      "Contact," "Lenore Bouchard," "Mallards in Winter,"
      "Saying Goodbye to Billy," "Too Late"
Christian Century: "Time of White Ice"
Coastal Plains Poetry: "Pine Missiles," "Skid Row"
Cold Mountain Review: "Skipping Stones"
The Comstock Review: "Postcard from Verona," "Wherever
      you are, north of here"
Crucible: "Hawk," "The Ice-Carver," "Ice Storm," "White
      Oak Creek, Westward" (Sam Ragan Poetry Prize)
Free Lunch: "CEOs," "Pegasus," "Playing with Lightning,"
      "Remembering Carla Hart in 1948," "Too Old for Vicky"
Iodine Poetry Journal: "At the Party"
Journal of The American Medical Association: "Selectivity"
KaKalaK Anthology of Carolina Poets (anthology): "The
      Forever Poem" (2008), "Doing the Box Step" (2009),
      "Genesis" (as "Credo" 2013), "Thin Air" (2017)
Main Street Rag: "Westwood Village, 1949," "Bracing
      Weather," "Higher Learning,: "Tennessee Night Fire,"
      "At the neighborhood homeowners' meeting"
The Moonwort Review, "Dreaming Astronomy"
New Orleans Review, "Perhaps"
Pembroke Magazine: "Backyard Music," "Testosterone in
      1943"

Pine Mountain Sand and Gravel: "Thinking of the Buddha
 at Pebble Creek"
Pinesong: The North Carolina Poetry Society (anthology):
 "Afterimage," "Bristlecone," "Burr Oak, Iowa—1853,"
 "The Dance," "Illusion," "New Issues," "Red Poppy,"
 "Remember," "Requiem," "Reveille," "Sailing," "Survival"
Poets for Peace (anthology): "Bracing Weather"
RATTLE: "At the Spring," "Buddhist Pigeon"
Sea, Sand and Sail: A Poetry and Prose Anthology: "Pier and
 Ocean"
Ship of Fools: "Montebello Night, 1951," "Class Photograph"
Slipstream,: "Carburetor Man"
Southern Poetry Review: "Greening"
Tar River Poetry: "From the Waiting Room Window"
Wellspring: "Old address book," "Tux Rental"

CHAPBOOKS
The Flower Sermon: "Requiem"
Genes: "Too Late"
The Ice-Carver, Longleaf Press at Methodist College:
 "The Ice-Carver"
Negotiating Physics and Other Poems: "Brownie"
 "Forest," and "Lochmere Lake"

Contents

Out After Dark

Detained by the Authorities

Light Sweet Crude

Continents of Light

The Girl Who Came Out with the Stars

The Flower Sermon

The Ice-Carver

Poets Anonymous

Negotiating Physics

Soledad

New Poems

Out After Dark

Quartzsite Arizona Night

We stopped at Quartzsite on the Yuma road
to camp overnight, bound for Mexico. Then
as the sun sank into far hills and distant cities
winked out into dark,
       we were left
under the diamond roof of night wind
too bright for sleeping.

       We tended Bedouin fires
that long night—on an island in the universe—
hugged the precious Earth with hip-holes
for our sleeping bags in the river sand and looked up
at the great cities of light wheeling over us.

Our records show
we made the trip to Mexico—I can't remember it,
but after all these years I am sometimes awakened
by those teeming stars.

Sonoita, Mexico—1952

Warm planetarium night.
The curtain of stars falls
to the desert floor
this side of *Cerro Pincate*—

black hills lashed
by ironweed, mesquite
boiling in night wind

wild wind kissing
Palo Verde trees awake,
reciting diamond

sutras of stars.
I dream, eyes wide
to night.

In the river sand
I feel a storm
five days away.

Death Valley February

We shed the muffler in Afton Canyon
& racketed the Merc into Furnace Creek,
arriving after dark. Stan & his buddy
shaved in warm radiator water & went

to some dance a sandstorm away
in Rhyolite. They rolled in after midnight,
still having a good time, voices high
& hooty, making lovesick coyote talk,

so I left them & roamed the moon-
flooded valley, night whispering
shy gusts, warm secrets,

walking the moon under earthshine
from Daylight Pass to Shoshone
looking for something I left behind.

Wherever you are, north of here

awake in the dark
to an orchestra of trees,
long strides of thunder
like a fast freight coming—
Midnight Special
making the bed rails sing,

I think of you
surfacing from sleep and how
it's too late to run
from the sweeping cross-hairs
of time and place, the bridge
dividing death from life
where lightning hasn't struck yet

and how we are both alive
in this moment,
listening.

Ice Storm

Only as far as the light
I walked into the hissing sleet,
pines like burdened mourners
bent. I thought of *Kristallnacht*,
Night of Broken Glass, its shards
lining defeated streets.
Hours ago I practiced the Mendelssohn
and was ready, but the rehearsal

was called off—the rehearsal you spoke of
when I first heard on the phone
your voice and knew how Lazarus felt
at the sound of his name
and the dazzling light.

How can there be winter
where you are? I look into the gray
of flying ice and wonder
how a voice could flood this house
with such abundant light.

Night of the Starlings

Sea-house porch. Night wind
rocks the empty chairs. Great stars
ride their rivers of light.

The children are all in from the sea.
Sand-pails are all put away.
In my country of sleep, Four-o-Clocks

that closed twelve colors tight
in the leeward yard pop and bloom
from Roman candles on the pier.

Awake in the dark to flying sand, I think
of the starling nests that sway
on the Ocean Avenue traffic lights.

Ready to depart, the house creaks
and counts its passengers. The starlings
have flown through a hole in the sky.

Campfire

Night fire near Lost River
San Joaquin South Fork.
No universe outside that light.
A Donner Party ghost
floated out in white,
led us in *Kumbaya*.

Her duet partner was drunk
on Old Spice aftershave
so they called me to the plank
to sing *Rose Marie* with her
up into the blaze of stars,
soap-scent of her in white, trees
looking about to catch fire.

The campfire burned out.
The spirit married the drunk
to save him. Years later
I went back to that charred circle
and after midnight heard a park ranger
tell a ghost story a lot like mine.

Time of White Ice

Eternal ice, vast windless
chill. Clear arctic waters'
quiet light. All night

the stars and lacquered
branches burned. All leaf
and berry of the holly white.

Again the ancient signal
has gone out and somewhere
in the night star-followers embark.

(And You, Creator, Child,
Comforter, again I feel the beating
of Your fetal heart).

Into a night of need for gifts
in myrrh and aloes wrapped we slept
until the ticking of some clock

or summer dream stirred ice
set off a rooftop avalanche.
Clear light of morning shows

three trees against the sky
in whitened silence—world
bundled in the stuff of light.

Detained by the Authorities

Origin of Species

Beside me, a Nobel physicist
is at his lunch, hard at his work
inspecting minute chunks of pork
like an obsessed pathologist.

I've seen raccoons work this way
and once I saw a chimpanzee
peel a banana with intensity
as if he were a beast of prey.

But this is our Professor Bright
who's mastered Kant's *Critique auf Deutsch*
but holds that Joyce says just as much
and quotes from *Finnegan's Wake* each night.

I wonder what Darwin might have found
if he had skipped the Beagle's cruise
in search of evolution's clues—
if he'd stayed home and looked around.

Professor Bright's right here to show
just how far an ape can go.

CEOs

Tall tan guys
from Yale with handicaps

of 5 & yacht club memberships.
More interchangeable than clones,

these chairmen, bred for generations
by The Best of Families.

They table-hop from board to board
with eastern seaboard smiles

they wear in sleep. Their gazes crinkle
at the corners of bronze squints

(consigning you & all your lineage
in squat flat to hell) as they go on

smiling in your face & downsize you
with those eyes.

Remember

when we rode the River Queen
down the Big Sandy
from Twelve-Pole Creek

and a hung-over church organist, Windy
Skeens, clambered up the cabin roof,
sat down at a battered red-and-gold

steam calliope and slammed out "Stars
and Stripes Forever" with masterful flourish
and so loud, cows fled the river banks

and people waved white flags from the shore
and you said to me, "Honey, there's the guy
I want to have play for us at our wedding."

Dreaming Astronomy

A wind came up in a dream
& blew me down warm night aisles
of twinkling houses with dioramas
of families reading their star-charts,

ticketed, packed & ready to go.
Overhead, a white hole opened
and a galaxy of winged astronomers
sprouted from its singularity to dance

       around the lights of autumn—
       Deneb, Vega, Altair. The Astronomer
       Royal put on his crown
& sat down in Cassiopeia's Chair.

I ran inside a planetarium just as its stars were
coming out, but an X-ray quasar chased me
into the African Room of a haunted museum
where zebras roamed from scene to scene

& impalas bounded away from the glass.
One lonely egret flew into a pink sunset
& I spun out into a starry place again.
All the October families had flown

to summer in Punta Arenas, under
the Southern Cross. High above, autumn's
lights were gone & the astronomers danced
around Bellatrix, Rigel & red Aldebaran.

At the neighborhood homeowners' meeting

last night, I noticed you
in your PTA wire-rims and
concerned-citizen tie. As I listened

carefully to your remarks,

your image—shit head—bloomed
before me like a Polaroid.

As you continued our enlightenment,
considering scenarios A, B, and C
I thought upon death

and life, and values blown
and the Giants-Cubs game I was
missing, and felt a sense of shame

for such judgment of another
who should be born again
with sufficient oxygen.

How to Become a Missing Person

The hero in the cartoon jail
sketches a door on the wall,
turns the knob and walks away.

I want to write night wind
and stars, rainsound,
sun-fragrant sage—that way,

to code the scent of orchards
on a page, or Christmas
when your hands made angel

shadows in the hall. Then
when that world's complete—I'll step
through into it. That real.

At the Party

tonight, Aunt Ethel, 123,
stroked her pale jade-colored necklace,
the green mamba about her throat,
as she tells Bill Phipps, my match-play
opponent tomorrow, how he will
beat me 3 and 2.

It's often like this—dreams in which
I know I'm dreaming, but can't wake up.
And the dead are always prophesying
and, of course, are never wrong.

Tonight, in living color, we have
another false democracy in which
the living should show a little more
respect, the dead, a little less familiarity.

In the dim bedroom, a seedy pianoman
bangs out Erroll Garner in the corner
while the rest smoke foul Gauloises
and make cocktail-talk as if I'm not there.

      Then they scare the hell out of me.
Waking on the bedside floor, I remember
how the lights flashed on and off
and they all came up and thanked me
for bringing them together for the last time.

Around the Campfire

The MFAs were camping out under the stars,
trying to keep a small fire going. They looked pale and
unhealthy in the moonlight. I walked up, uninvited,
and sat down. After a while, one of them read a post-
language sonnet, and the next one, a post-structuralist
villanelle, which the others had memorized because
they all joined in, chanting the final stanza. There was
a period of silence, then a flurry of talk about the
impact of post-deconstructionist minimalism upon the
New York School. Then it was my turn. The magic of
the moon and the night was upon me and I read my
prize-winning "Rondeau for Air-Pump and Teakwood
Hammers." There was a long silence, then the apparent
leader of the group spoke. "That showed some
elements of literacy," he said.

The Forever Poem

Again it's light—
an unspoiled day.
All the bad choices,
the sins
have not yet kicked in.

The world seems to be running
smoothly without me.
The morning paper has not yet
arrived to tell me
what to be upset about.
The Flicker happily drums
the rain gutter without my instructions.

All praise
to the rumbling forced-air furnace,
the coffee maker (burbling to life)
to the growling stomach
of my cat (black velvet nose
prodding me for tuna).

All praise to the self-reliant miracles
everywhere, spared in these early
moments of befuddlement,
from my stupendous power
to screw them up.

Soon, I will thrust my hand back into
the watch-works of creation,
gum-up a dozen wonders—
but for now, a determined ant

trudges the ceiling above me.
Tomorrow will come, and once more
the world will wait for me
to sleep
so it can heal.

Light Sweet Crude

Sanders Transfer

Charleston, West Virginia, 1959

Ace Stonebreaker drove the big white
Sanders truck down from Skitter Creek
and parked out front. He & three derelict hulks
in undershirts & shiny pants got out
& climbed the steps. Lonnie, the ugliest,
reverently pointed out the boss, a little man
in a wide-brim black hat. "That there's Mr. Ace.
Why he could dang near move that there piana
up them stairs by hisself."

Lonnie, Buzz & Tooth-Pick
white gristle top to toe. Tooth-Pick belly-bumped
the fridge into the truck while Buzz & Lonnie
tossed sofas like toys. Worked fast & not
a scratch. Come five o'clock the boss hollered
"Let's go, boys, we got a right fur piece to go up Elk
while good daylight holds." Tooth-Pick allowed
"A leetle brown jug go right nice 'bout now."
Word of mouth. No *Yellow Pages*. Customer satisfaction.

Warning Signs

Entering the Wild & Wonderful
West Virginia Turnpike, south
of Princeton, I am cautioned by these signs:

INGLESIDE EXIT—NO REENTRY
      north-bound (going north)
      south-bound (going south)

From the road, I can't see a town, but
there may be cars & people in there,
trapped since it was built,
like grape seeds in a bad appendix.
Since then, how many
unsolved disappearances?

Maybe Ingleside collapsed
into a car black hole.
Spinning round & round
in that NASCAR cyclotron,
De Sotos, finned like the triceratops,
Hudsons—howling 85 in second,
Nashes—floored and roaring to escape
& Edsels with their grilles—
those fabled silver toilet seats—
forever orbiting.

Carburetor Man

The Chevy coughed, sucked wind
& died as we rolled into Peters
Feed & Automotive, four miles south
of Clarkton, NC, Ball-Peen, the counter

man, said, "Sounds like the carb,
I'll go fetch Slim." They shoved tires
aside & raised the hood. Men ringed
the hanging 60-watt bulb to watch

The Carburetor Man. Slim laid white
stud-dealer's hands on the greasy
steel throat, yelled, "Crank the sucker,"
& flapped in gas. Then he scooped

deep with a skinny tool for the uvula
(or whatever the hell is down there)
and tweaked some screws. From a Pepsi
bottle marked NITRO, Slim poured

down a chaser & goosed the jets. The Chevy
roared! Eighteen bucks for the ring-side
seat, but our tee-time had passed.
So we stayed the night for the tractor-pull.

Selectivity

Where thalamic clavichords have
keys uncountable, only spidery hands
can finger major, minor—a third

from joy to blue, a fifth from rose
to sky. A single hydrogen may
hold the right key down, a methyl—

turn the night sky green. Once
ham-fisted phenothiazines slammed
out cacophonies like diskinetic

drunks at a karaoke bar, thick fingers
beating joy with pain. Now
nanobot Perahias slip blood/brain

fences unescorted, pump serotonin
yo-yos between synaptic paddles
until a side-man flips a switch,

sends voltages to keyboards and mixers
down the line. Pure frequencies.
For the music, details we needn't know.

An Outdoor Wedding

When the Sacred Heart Church caught fire
the wedding was moved to the parish garden
under the smoking olive trees
where the bride's and groom's families
waited, toasting marshmallows over the blaze.
The big red diocesan fire truck showed up
and Kevin O'Connor and Marco Salvino
pumped secular water onto the inferno,
flames leaping from the vats of holy oil
and other spirituous liquors set alight.

Arriving late to the wedding,
I relieved myself in the parish house restroom,
lost in an old-growth forest
of priests lined up at urinals,
their lemony streams turning pinot noir
from the transubstantiation there.

It was a wedding to remember.
Everyone said there had been
a miracle, for the new wine wasn't
watery at all. The assembled clergy,
vestments sweaty from the pep rally for Saint
Jodocus, patron against fire, and wearied
from the massive miracle performed,
held the new couple to be especially blessed,
and the wine a full-bodied noir,
rivaling the best outputs of all the friars of France.

Boardinghouse Blues

Returning late, you are apt to see
Aunt Emma waiting up for you
in her high lace collar & high-backed chair.
      As you climb the stair
old fragrances of supper rise. Below,

Old Billy rumbles in his room
alone with his Dixieland radio,
takes his suspenders down.
(Regulars still out on the town).

Outside, the night streets
smell of lilac & nowhere to go.
      You wonder
where the world is going, if at all
& pass Aunt Em,
reading about some funeral.

The Ancient Chorister

The old guy with his nose
full of Vick's has a voice
like a moose in full cry

and breath like an opened grave
but they let him sing
the Messiah year after year.

For His acceptable praise,
God calls up all His instruments—
even the old man,

like a taped-up gym piano
with broken, blackened keys
still an authentic musical species.

He dons his robe again and sings
(and Handel smiles, directing
            from the wings).

To Hell with Science

I don't like the "weather" channel
on TV. Surprises are for me—
weather, for example,
or Santa Claus
or Death.

It's better not to know
a heart-attack is just
around the corner.

I like surprises: knowing that
would spoil the fun.

I'm going out now & sniff
the night sky, smell the grass,
the glittering stars, listen
to wind rustle the locust trees.

I know winter is coming
like hemorrhoids & death,
I know it's going to snow—
a white Christmas or
my car over a guard-rail.
But I'm going in now & drink
a Budweiser. The hell with TV.

I'm going back
to the Almanac.

I don't want radar telling me
the front has reached Greensboro,
the clock is running.
120 miles/40 mph = 3 hours away.

Higher Learning

Montebello, California, 1943

The word was
the Red Raiders would
meet us under
the Bella Vista water tower
at ten o'clock that night
to settle things, so
all day in Mr. Ratchitt's
metal shop

we made knucks
of cold rolled steel
leaving the edges
burred. But somebody
tipped the cops
and that night, ten or so
showed up in squad cars
with blue spotlights
along with a few parents

and a church camp
counselor with bibles
and a stack of pamphlets
on healthy activities
for the young.
And that was that.

Continents of Light

Skipping Stones

I didn't mean to eavesdrop
but their voices startled me
from far across the lake. I hope

my thoughts reach you this way
sometimes, like pagan prayers
distracting you in mid-breath,

soft as the touch of a stranger
in a crowd. buried in chaos,
my signature for you.

   You are so far away—
across miles of night
and family privacy. If only
there were this lake

and nothing else between us
I could skip my words
across to you like stones.

Moonstone Beach, Oregon, to Punta Arenas, 3:15 a.m.

Brown hair—fragrance of inland
wild mustard—tonight you read
Sun Yun Feng to me and we gather

star clusters from her *River of Heaven*.
Tonight, I can remember innocence
tonight, I can say anything to you.

Now by a silent Ferris wheel, we stroll barefoot,
too light to sink in hourglass sand. South of Carmel
we walk on moon-mirrors where the surf runs

back, your face sky-bright in playa spray.
We chase our shadows into silver foam
then join a whirl of dancers circling

eucalyptus smoke of beach-fires in the wind.
Now we have drifted into southern waters
I cannot name the stars. I must go down

the vine of dreams to day.
(South of Rosarita Beach
ensueño is the word for dream.)

Brown hair—write to me
one line from Rio, or the Azores
or the Land of Fire

Lenore Boucher

In the ninth grade, Lenore
looked twenty, beautiful sophisticate
and with a name like French perfume
we fantasized things she must be doing
in ways of Parisian grace.

That first dance at Eastmont Junior High,
shy boys huddled along the wall,
drones waiting for their queen,
Lenore came over, invited each of us
in turn to dance, and we danced with her
in the veil of her grace, senses
flooded and stopped at a time
for later looking, that dance a movie
we ran many times. Why did she do this?

Last week I dreamed of Lenore
alone at dawn, dancing by an ocean.
She saw me, came across the pale sand
and spoke, words lost in sea-sound.
She ran to the surf, floated
in arabesque, a gull against the wind.
Then I lost her in a tide of light.

Mirella

The hanging glasses make a chandelier
above her and she is aquavit, maraschino,
Bombay Sapphire. In the bar mirror

she is unreal. She bends for Bushmills
and my nitroglycerine heart
signals danger. They say she takes

the back door of rough trade. They laugh
and say she goes down hot
like good whiskey. Let the loafers,

swillers of cheap beer talk and roll
up their hopes like dimes. Let them
remember her in black, her time of tears,

the red votives lit by her mother's
good girl. When the floor is cleared,
chairs and tables set aside, she is the one

I will ask for the next dance—
the "Delirium Waltz," to sweep her
out into its great arc under the stars.

Afterimage

After Diabelli's Mass in F-Maj, December, 1994

Long after you have gone
concert over, crowd gone home
                                        your face

still lights this room

like the moon above
a veil of clouds.
                              I wait

in my seat while it lasts.
I turn to watch the foyer

for you to reappear, angel
out of nothing, bearing your

                    incredible light

to speak my name (your sound
like no other sound). To make

the room and night and all its faces
disappear.

What does it matter

if the other singers see me
scan the room for you,
hoping for a chance to speak,

if the director remembers
that I always ask
about your absence,

if the others notice
when I walk with you
to your car? What does it matter

and who will care?
May has a way
of becoming November.

Each time I climb the stairs
to the music
there is less of me

for discussion. So catch me
out. Let me betray
one small quirk of the living.

Doing the Box Step

It was the music that started him.
Every day, as the last
of the lunch crowd exited the elevator
in the forty-story on East Main,
he couldn't keep his feet still.
No room for a samba, but the box step
was made for the eight-by-eight floor.

When the door hushed shut
and George Winston played on,
he had only to start slow-dancing
in a square and she would be in his arms,
auburn pageboy, blue blue eyes,
her warm breath grazing his ear
with the deliciousness

of getting away with it, as if
in a Rolls' leather back seat. Always
the possibility of an angry husband
waiting at the next floor.
Always the rush of speeding up to
the unexpected, the plunge
that would take her breath away.

Illusion

Bird
        broken against
               my window
flew into illusion
hard against reality

as in my poem
flown to you
        hard against you

leaving part of me
on the glass.

Angel

You, consort of stars,
vaulter of night's light ages,

arrived on Earth to card
melodies from the babble of rivers,

and attend my beginnings.
You visited

my parents' rooms when their voices
rose through the walls and spelled

their quarrels into tenderness.
How often have you fended

my prayers, giving me more?
Were you the stranger who spoke

my name in a foreign city
where no one knew me? Lax creditor

forgiving debts I would forget,
you reward my doubt

and answer my impudent questioning
with ravishing mysteries.

When a sudden storm blinded
the house lights and wind pounded

the kitchen door, I was the child
who invited you in.

Moment Musicale

For the Charleston Civic Chorus, Charleston, West Virginia

Rewinding time to some realm
lost in universes past
Authur Drake, recording expert,
has not yet accidentally erased
my *Three Sundays of a Poet* tape.

                  He shuffles
into the choir room
with his standard fifty dollars
of loose change ajingle, but who can tell
because we're practicing
Stravinsky's *Symphony of Psalms*
which even when sung right

                      sounds wrong
(though who can tell
because we never sang it right).
And I could look through all
past universes, find the same.

But right now Drake is safely
silver-weighted to his chair,
my tape will live another hour
(I think I'll rest right here).

To Lo Yin: In Memoriam

The daughter of Cheng' Tien fell in love with the poetry of Lo Yin, but after seeing the poet's ugly face would never read his work again.

—Five Dynasties Period

October

Ugly or not, what does it matter
now that what was once your face
are only ashes in my hands?
I still recall your words
of an inner place brighter than the flame
of chrysanthemum. And now those words
alone are left for us:
and I, daughter of Cheng' Tien,
an old maid thankful for quietude,
wait in the shade of moonlight,
waiting for memories, not sleep.
I have slept enough of life away.

April

White storm of hawthorn petals
in the April wind recalls to me your words
with colors for each change of heaven.
How was I so blinded by my youthful eyes,
shocked by your ill-made face,
I shunned your words as blasphemy?
Your lines have long outlived
that tragedy and my old eyes
now see more clearly in their loneliness.

Your words are all I have now of you
and my soul's prayer is to meet
at last and twine with yours
in the willowed vault of paradise.

Moonrise

White goddess, sweet wanderer
of dark, again I celebrate
your quiet rise, at once a nocturne
and a catch of sorrow in the throat
of night. I pray

       that you would fill
all space made vacant by our loss,
would heal, with your strange innocence,
our frenzy and despair.

As you slip the hills, I give
into your keep all estranged
from love, all exiled from hope,
who no longer look for your return.

I ask you to remember
Mother, Father, me someday
when I have escaped

through your bright window
into the seas and continents of light.

The Girl Who Came Out
with the Stars

Westwood Village, 1949

It's nighttime and I'm in somebody's apartment near the UCLA campus. The noisy, half-lit room is full of people at some kind of student-faculty affair. We're all sitting on the floor, though there are chairs, because that's the kind of party it is. It's a time before we even thought of smoking pot.

I feel that the most important event of my life is about to take place. I'm drinking a coke with the girl with the world's greatest legs and auburn hair. She has just refused to marry me. A young bearded prof from the Caltech history department sits to my left, his back against the wall. He sings, in a deep deep basso, "If I Had the Wings of an Angel." I'm stunned he can sing like that. I envy his existence and would envy it, even if I knew he were to fall down a mountain tomorrow. He is back from a year's study with the Lamas in Tibet and has no need for girls with the greatest legs because he has gotten beyond all that. I'm hoping I can find this guy if I am ever in need. As long as I can find him, everything, even with the leggy auburn girl, will turn out fine.

Class Photograph

It is a poor photo, gray and grainy
like an old war-time picture,
eleventh-graders rounded up, faces
like eggs in a box, but I can always find her,
three rows down from the white-
T-shirt boys in black jackets
twelfth from the end she stands
in a life I wish she could live again

Did the photographer ever see that face,
worried look straight out, dark hair
against her white blouse, for just one time
the body as the soul made visible?
So remote from any commitment
of the flesh—in that simple frame
of white—not by her wish
a part of me.

—italicized line from *The Trail of the Sandhill
Stag*, Ernest Thompson Seton

Pier and Ocean

I remember the pier
winding like Draco into the stars
     where we walked far
      into the sounding night
        Then awake
to the morning wind, sailing
bright water off Carmel
into your azure latitudes
my hand on the tiller, yours
on the sail.

     Stella Maris—Star of the Sea
you were that day, Pacific
calm at your command,
far water awake and rolling
like a wheat field in the wind
and your eyes deep
in the hue of ocean and heaven.

Once,

before you
became
disenchanted with

my performance
as a human
being, a moment

moon-filled came
when you,
disabled by

my suave façade
& stunned
into foolish

extravagance,
called me
angel.

Montebello Night, 1951

Odor of night-blooming jasmine
brings her back, star-shadow
of her hair sways on the door.

Mixed night chorus—tree frogs, crickets
fill our silence of goodbye.

Eyes dark in starlight,
she waits, forever twenty-two
wherever jasmine blooms.

Evocation

Magician of recalling, I hunt for you
under the horn-moon when you vanish

around sycamores at the corners of sight.
Once you were a rowdy carousel. When you

became a goddess I waited for you to come
round like a legendary star to enter

and graze in the garden I made for you,
your tall silhouette against my fence.

I saw your face and became who I am,
but you became veiled beyond describing.

I know you cannot promise to return,
but for a lifetime your wildness calls me back.,

a fragrance startling under the birches.
I lie in wait for you beside streams, listen

for your footsteps' echo in sandstone canyons.
I exhaust your hiding places. I wait for the night

of nights when you will show yourself to me,
if only distant at the edges of sleep.

Too Old for Vicky

Always just out-of-reach
she never seemed to touch ground—
like a bright swallowtail,

too lovely to be real.
Much too young to date that man,
Barbara, her sister, worried.

I have lost the color
of her eyes, but I remember green
water filling her footprints

in the surf at Montego Bay
and her sister's words—now
that Vicky has been taken

beyond all nights and assignations.
Taken to the bosom of one
much too old for us all.

Afterward

If, by Jesus magic,
I should be roused from the dark
Sargasso of time, if I should awake
in the bright surprise of forever and find you—
you who shunned all magic,
and despite your unbelief, a girl,
pride of your father, your mother's eyes,
then stunned by the girl of flowered dresses
I once pushed in a playground swing,

would I remember the time when I asked
only to be gathered into the rich mortality
of your life, to be carried along with your
remaining days, from the lighted porch,
and the Christmas I spent with your family
instead of mine, when I wished
to surrender to the blue flags of your eyes,
to vanish with you downriver
to wherever you go?

The Flower Sermon

Backyard Music

Back in the California
of old Sawtelle, West L.A.,
beehive radios & screen porches,
we were awakened at 2:00 a.m.
by a party next door at the Roses.
Their party jumping like a Model A
on three cylinders, they wrestled
the piano into their backyard &
invited the world of 1936.

       Our sleep was shattered,
we were outraged, complained.
Sixty-one years ago, the Roses'
drunken revel, doing something
we would never do, so undignified,
       rude, outrageous.
What a fabulous idea!

Tux Rental

For Dick Bernhard, keeper of the legend

Loan, actually. At all-male Caltech
In the 50's, you could get decked-out
For the spring Scripps dance, no charge

At the suit shack back of the cafeteria.
They came in midnight black or gray
With fins like '59 De Sotos, doublewide &

Prison striped. Moths never made the holes
We found. The story was that the mob
Of coats & pants had been salvaged

From the St. Valentine's Day Massacre or
Possibly after the following funeral,
Trouser creases pressed to Sicilian razors

& stains steamed out. On the dance floor,
My girl gave the huge suit elaborate room
Then hung on the lapels, admired the great fit

Across the back & laughed. Not me.
For once I was the master of situations
Displayed at social ease, in the right place

At the right time, impeccably attired.
Not bad, on top of knowing we would drive
Back later through the scent

Of the orange trees, that we would all
Live in Bel Air someday—live forever
With Palm Springs in our backyard

Between the ski-slopes and the surf,
Our loved-ones all alive & no cup
Ever allowed to go below half-full.

Greening

The way wild grape climbs to screen
the lightning-shattered oak,
the way orchard grass flushes
against a crumbled wall
is like a watercolor finishing itself,
wet-brushing from all its borders in.

Man-made things invite wild art.
Greenbrier topples rusted flue-cure shacks
and kudzu plunges down roadside culverts
south of Mocksville, scales signs with names
like Yadkin and Uwharrie. Even wheel-tracks
at a burned out feed-lot vanish,
reappear as fireweed, columbine.

Here, on the road-crew's trim,
woodbine resumes its patient overgrowth.
If I should look for this place
a week from now, I'd never find it
amid the many baffling shades of green
the hue of everything to be.

Mallards in Winter

With the leaves down, I see them
paddle the creek, green heads
against the lighted flow.

They drift downstream in silence,
as if in a painting on a silk screen,
toward Lake of the Winds.

Their wakes show them to be real.
I watch them bob and disappear,
then emerge from the banks into the winter's

silvering light. They let the current
take them, soundless, through
the shadowed channel's mystery.

Their peace is so profound I cannot
disturb them. Their house is icebound,
but its attic is the sky. In the tearing storms

I invite them to take refuge in my dreams.
At the canvas edge, where the seasons
change, they escape into springtime.

At the Spring

Before she could drink
from the garden hose,
a cardinal landed on her wrist

and plunged its beak into the clear
bubbling. She froze in the scarlet
presence, but managed to gentle

the nozzle's flow. Never so close
to a wild thing, she was soaked
but held rock-still as the redbird

clung to her wrist, tilting its head
up and down as it drank, so close
she could see its tiny tongue.

There was a song—whether in her
stunned mind, or from a distant
questioning bird, she could not tell.

For a moment, nothing died.
For a moment, the winds lost their ways.
The hose chirred softly

like a night thing's call, the redbird
lisping as it dipped,
again and again, into the spring.

Red Poppy

Sovereign and free
as geese rising to the stars, finale

of all arguments for God,
I have seen Him light
a darkened room

with the bright incarnation
of your smile.

         Now
in the shadowed concert hall
you are white
as a desert lily in the night.

You are a forest fire
inside me, you are the blood-
red poppy.

Buddhist Pigeon

On the Bangkok sidewalk, it pecks
a pink gum-smear.
If it has a soul, it's a crapshoot
whether
its karmic trip is going
up or down. If souls go down,
they may get very small or
have no size at all,
unthinkable as the primordial
zero universe which we
believe, but can't conceive.
In theophysics séance parlors,
one may posit various houses
for the soul, Buddhist, Christian,
otherwise, then ask how
Soul traffics with the Mind
(which I've always pictured as
a skull-sized synthesizer hitched
to Yeats' *dying animal*).
            Perhaps
our pigeon's soul is a
Heifitz of whatever
instruments its journey
takes it through. It may be limited
and singular, lingering beneath
the mauve and lice-infested wings
to animate the worm-brained
bird, or vast and multiple, navigating
flocks in flight. Suppose

his soul is indivisible,
smaller that the smallest thing
and made of nothing else. Finally

it *slips like a dewdrop into the shining sea.*
Each of us—worm, bird or me
just a blink of the brightest light.

Old address book

kept too long, so many names crossed out,
phone numbers like weathered dates on stones,
addresses X'd and gone. Such simple cancellation

of lives. I'm afraid to call the old numbers left,
no way to prepare for what I might find after
these years—the sorrow, resentment caught

off-guard, my voice too high and eager,
a curious intruder come back to unearth you
from some place you'd rather be. Or worse—

to dial up an irritated stranger, your familiar sound
gone like a stone into the sea, showing
how we are all so interchangeable. Listen—

if my voice breaks, it's not from curiosity
but fear—that you are gone. I only want
to find you as you were. And so I will write

again, hoping this year you will answer.
That, like me, you will find the safe ground
of written words between us. If only I could

tell you how some word or glance of yours
once grew in me, became part of what I am.
You will never know the way you are alive in me.

Thinking of The Buddha at Pebble Creek

Cary, North Carolina

I picture him here, far from his forest gathering,
where this stream washes its pebbles white. Gautama,

deliverer from sorrow, stands facing the bridge
in the clearing as his hearers walk away.

The dogwoods are long past, but goldenrod flares
saffron in the shadows. The flower he held

in silence has fallen to the path.
How could he have guessed that one would understand

and carry that silence to all who listen,
like a great tide circling and re-circling the world?

The Ice-Carver

The Ice-Carver

On the promenade deck
of the M/S Tropica, the ice-carver
works against the clock. Intent
as Donatello, he chips into
the block, releasing the falcon
flying from the soft blue stone.
He moves swiftly over the ice,
the gathered crowd already
losing focus, melting away
to the next entertainment.

His work complete, the carver
steps back, brushing ice-chips
from his beard. In the cloud-light
he could be a young Buonerotti,
chiseled fragments in his dark hair,
recalling David's liberation from
his white stone.

Already the falcon's wings are wet
but will carry it until the bell
for lunch calls the stragglers away.
A movement in the melting mirror
catches the carver's eye—
a white seabird vanishing.
The carver's message passes
like a poem never written down.

New Issues

Waiting in the post-office queue
for the *Virgin and Child* Christmas stamp,
I see the Enrico Fermi issue on display.
The Roman physicist, like a Moses of our age,
chalks revelations on his slate, *carbon*—
star-forged alpha of our flesh, and with us
escaping into space and time. He smiles,
pleased to share good news. I feel
December's chill bite from the swinging door.

Lorenzo Costa's portrait on the other stamp
has caught the blue-clad mother and her babe
in a moment of unlikely serenity. How far
we have travelled since Lorenzo's day!
In the darkening chill, I would return
to his three-tiered world, to cloak myself
against the winds of space in folds of the *Pietà*,
find refuge in gentle Mary's flowing folds,
bound for whatever awaits beyond the stars.

Perhaps

Someone in the photo who looks like me
climbs a spring-wet trail to Alta Peak,
wild columbine—five colors
against the sky. I was never there.

I never swam with Carl at Heather Lake.
Nor was I in Florence—the Ponte Vecchio
in that picture through a rainy mist.

Perhaps I hold memories until
what happened never happened at all—
maybe time abolishes time.

I think of East L.A. thirty years ago—
the TV is on and Dad falls asleep in front
of company. That's where I never was
so often now.

But those photographs! Two boys
bobbing in some mountain lake—sun
in their eyes, the moment drifting
like cloud-shadows over the water.

Pegasus

The horse rears skyward as she hugs
his back, nears the live oak's lower
branches. The girl is lost in transport
as she takes the great surge

between her legs. The menace
of trees and ground are only colors
now—dun of road dust, forest green—
fear cancelled by the moment's shine.

So begins their first long gallop.
Ektachrome 200 shows only a girl
flying on a white-tailed colt. What was it
her mother warned her of?

Horse and girl have found a trail
her mother has forgotten
and follow a river whose rising
she will not see again.

Skid Row

In front of a cheap hotel
the old man takes out his baggage
in the yellow light—an ex-boxer
or waiter or retired pioneer
with that unmistakable
blunt athletic confidence,
dressed for some personal rodeo,
showing the street he is still alive.

Here, old men die in winter
but blue buses pull across the scene.
If there were lights and blankets,
they are gone—
the love & food & church parade moves on.
      Today,

more men are missing
at roll-call on the street
and have gone somewhere to wear
their red ties and Sunday best.

In October

afternoons, sun warms
a hot spice-smell in the wind
that quits quick and clean
as a promise broken.

Only   this instant is real
in the warm and light
and the next also
when it comes.

Wind comes and goes
and shows you
(more than you want)
how every waking moment
is goodbye.

Postcard from Verona

Under the Via Capello archway
to the balcony of Juliet, in every color
of Verona, is a Sistine Chapel
of graffiti: *Baffy + Kurt Insieme,*
Benedetta, alone in blue,
Simona e Giani Forever, mixing
the languages in rose of Titian,
Fiorenza, in gold, *Fernando*
with stars.

       Someone named Carmina
has written:
            Ave mundi luminar
            Ave mundi rosa

I shine my flashlight
on a ceiling of the Vatican
torch-lighted. Here are no guards,
no hours of visit.

       Someone approaches.
       Her red dress rustles
       as she walks.

The wall is soft
to my felt-tip. It is like
marking on an arm.

Next

Even after good times funnel
down to intervals between waiting rooms
(for another report to set you free)

—you'll still come back for more.

After the fiftieth reunion
(where the class president went
unrecognized), you'll wait by your mailbox
for the Kodacolor souvenir.

Someday reprieves expire
and tomorrow becomes now.
Think of what your molecules have
always wanted and let them go.

Think of how easily TV strangers die
in distant lands. Where do all the people
come from who never heard of you?
How inexhaustible they are!

That's the secret. Think
of yourself as news
from a far country.

Poets Anonymous

Testosterone, 1943

Fall football at Montebello High,
blue & gold jerseys, boys in the stands
high on home-front hormones, lusting for war.
Stratton's peroxide hair turned purple,
Swede Metzenbaum's a royal bluing blue.
Henna'd mustaches, Rit-dyed sideburns flamed
in the sun and we'd sworp around the track
past the dames with their legs made-up, finger-salute
the visitor stands—Monrovia, Downey, East L.A.,
curse in bad street Spanish—*chingas tu madre!*
A brain-damaged gutter ball, Whitey Privette,
bowled guys down from behind & the crowd
surged to the parking lot for street-fighting room.

     Last game at Downey, Pete Marino led
the battle charge through the tennis courts
(past Linda Brown in her short white shorts).
Late 2nd half, two big pachucos
shouldered Pete back asleep, his war over,
stretched him on the asphalt, home again.

     Our hair grew out black, brown & blond,
combed into ducktails with Blue Waltz. Harry James
     broke his arm but his lip was fine. We stripped
all the chrome off '42 Chevys & dropped
their rear ends, racked their twin Smitties & lined 'em up
to drag Vail & Cleveland Streets after dark.

Playing with Lightning

We'd be like Ben Franklin
with his kite, two amateurs
in a thunderstorm. He was
damn lucky!—flew his line up

Lady Weather & she tickled
his key & sent him home unharmed.
It would be fun to find out
what it's like, just a tiny jolt,

then walk away & write it in
a diary & of course my scientific
curiosity is aroused. But old Ben
had quite a keyring &

a knack for tiptoeing & leaving
just in time. So what do you think
of the chances for both of us
to get away with it?

Sketch Belvedere

East Los Angeles, 1943

Once, Whittier and Atlantic Boulevards
marked the marketplace of dreams
called Belvedere, with its multiethnic ladies
and their multicolored hair.

The Armenian shoe store that fitted
me with stylish nineteen-forties gunboats
under orange lights is gone—melted
into sweaty creases of the urban map.

I still recall the glorious plum shade
of those shoes in daylight and how two
Zoot-Suiters eyed them longingly
before I reached my car.

Now relics in my attic, but still
brand-new, they blush lavender
beneath their dust, like old love couplets
never sent, nor meant for light of day.

Remembering Carla Hart in 1948

"Carlita Corazon" we called her
in our high school Spanish Club. We were
honor students and so enlightened
we wouldn't have jaywalked
without a committee decision.

But things happened fast one day
at Whittier and Atlantic Boulevard.
Too many piled into the old Ford
and Carla Hart jumped on my lap.
¡Ayee! ¡Caramba! I could only
hold her like Teresa of Avila,
and in the hormone storm
all I could do was sing!

Later, Carla broke the piñata
at the Spanish Club Christmas party.
It was the last time I ever saw her
and she left me with the taste
of bright red candy scattered everywhere.

Bracing Weather

Walked through an orange-grove
& came upon five men in baseball
caps hooting and stomping

like punk rock gods while two
indoctrinated roosters bloodied
each other with steel
spurs. Since wars began

old men have sent the young
away to die and we are both.
OK taxpayers, those warlords

of the chickenyard. We're all
hardwired with the hot red rooster
light—that sends us out to die.
The men bag up the casualties

& smooth out the ground. Marching
bands are like cocaine—they make
dread ecstasy & war a kind of weather

to survive, a few lives shed
for Glory. Never what it really is—
that happens to you & me alone
just one time, lights out, forever.

The Word from the Dumpster

He didn't look like a scientist—
more like the curator of a wax museum—
but the lanky stale hair, the morning
coat with frilled shirt
yellow as an ancient manuscript,
were vaguely musical—
a nineteenth-century piano tuner
or itinerant oboist. Probably
he'd just arrived from a night
in the dumpster he was walking from.

       We almost collided.
he stared at me—hard—pale gaze blazing
with some weird priority & said
"If you surrender to Jesus Christ
you will be released from the laws
of physics"—just like that—then vanished
down a side street. And I had to stop
& think what I was going to do about it
that Chicago April day.

Reveille

For John Dixon

Given his druthers, Lefty Beale
would have kept both hands, but
he grew right proud of the shiny
state-of-the-sixties gripper
they fitted him after

the lab explosion. Company to the bone
and son of a mine super who fought
the U.M.W., he wouldn't have sued
if F. Lee and all his crew
had parachuted in. And Lefty

       got to wear it
fishing trips where he roused us
before good daylight beating
that two-pound steel hook up
against the cabin door. After

the cancer ate away his soft
parts, he rose with that blinding
stainless crab and beat upon the gate
of New Jerusalem.
And they took him in.

Saying Goodbye to Billy

Once, Billy's gang dammed up
Jack's run, set things on fire,
looped snares for rabbits and built
tree houses in the woods, now
they've come to say goodbye

too late. Death is the ultimate
privacy. To each other
we, the living, bid farewell.

This is the picture Rockwell
never painted. Billy in makeup
receiving subjects, even
his mother. This comforts her.
He is far from here.

What can he know of this
in the clenched fist
of space and time?

He was thirty-six.
The boys who built tree houses
never saw their friend like this.
They edge into the room
before such majesty.

Sky Divers

"Everybody out."
At thirteen thousand feet
we jumped and made
our only perfect star

then shifted to survival.
Ripcords pulled,
all failed as one.

As only fact
can frustrate probability
we fell, all uninsured
toward our soft blue
home—drifting, then aimed
at a hard target,

our families picnicking,
unprepared for us.

Only Liang, the physicist,
smiled, Buddhistic

at his destiny, knowing
gravity is always
on the job.

Negotiating Physics

White Oak Creek, Westward

At N.C. Highway 751, White Oak Creek enters
a forest of flooded trees.

The light came in a dream. I followed
its pigeony flickers through nightgreen woods

to where it vanished in a waterfall.
Next day I found those trees, and a path

that took me over a tiny bridge where a worn board
banged and flushed a Great Blue from a minnow

pool. Delicate feet together, he spread blue vans
and floated into deeper green downstream.

I followed its counsel of sibilance westward
to a bend where White Oak Creek drains

basinward to the Cape Fear, then opens

to a forest of dead oak towers in the Lake Jordan
water-land. Acorn to sprout, their lives cast off
to pale heartwood. The heron was there.

Lochmere Lake

Cut stars
of *liquidamber* leaves
against the darkening sky.
In the Kingdom of Night
campgrounds of fireflies
weave light and shower

Luna in her mirror—
lake with stars. Sunken beacon
bobbing moon.

Does the perched kingfisher
know he is Archangel's
shadow?

Great blue heron, tall and still
finds safety with the geese
and ducks in dry dock,
a shipyard of them
in the dark—
at home.

Brownie

Part-sheltie prince of canine vagabonds
you showed up one day
and chose me. A dog and his boy
neither pedigreed, we borrowed summer
after golden summer, our bond unregistered
except by love.

      At the end
I carried you in a cardboard box
to a farm, by the Rio Hondo river,
that took pets for burial. Children came
from the farmhouse to look at you.
"Isn't he pretty," one of the girls said.

      You were a gypsy smelling summer,
why did you choose me for such lessons
of sorrow and great joy?

Deer Hunter

In easy range across the glade
a six-point white tail, robed in velvet—
intimate cloak of bare mortality,
paints me with his gaze.
       I remember
boyhood hunting days—
a casual Nimrod, armed
and licensed for the kill.
Providence always sent the deer
elsewhere, always sent me away
from one unhappy loss
of innocence.

Pine Missiles

Who has seen
pine needles fall
like elfin missiles
from the sky
to pierce the fat
magnolia leaves?

No one,

but in the dawn
I find them
where they fly.
Of this phenomenon
I ask, "How?" I ask
"is there a why?"

Burr Oak, Iowa—1853

Daylight fading, cold coming on,
their wagons pass through,
bumping on iron-rimmed wheels,
headed for Wyoming, Colorado, Utah.
Under the white chill of stars
they tether their stock by Silver Creek,
spread blankets on the courthouse lawn,
lie down under trees in front yards to sleep.
To be back home in Ohio, Indiana for a while.
Tonight, too tired to be my ancestors—
tonight, no answers for tomorrow.

       Far off—sheeps' bells stir
in the night wind. Far off drift of harmonica,
last one awake by his campfire on the *Long Trail
Winding*. West wind brings honeysuckle
from Fort Atkinson tomorrow. Wind makes
it harder to remember names left behind.

The harmonica player lets his fire die—
the stars will be their sentries.
He dozes and hears someone say,
we must never forget who we are.
Watch fires run low on wood. Above
the dark camps, faces of sons and grandsons
swirl in smoke rising to the stars.

Soledad

Survival

I am here
Or there, or elsewhere. In my beginning.

—T.S. Eliot

When I am gone
I will be behind a creosote bush,
deep in a Mojave arroyo
no one has ever seen. I will
still be aware—the awareness
of a desert hiker
who, turning toward the wind,
sees a saw-whet owl fly
from that arroyo
at a great distance.

Where are the nests of shadows?
In wastelands or lost farms
where you, hiker, casting out
your thoughts, will never go.
Silently, they climb the stairs
like tenants their landlord never sees.
They are more alive than memories,
        and when your thoughts stray
from grocery lists to flashes
of a stream or hidden field,
they've touched you.

The owl tacks windward.
Deep in the canyon wildness
her fledglings wait for food.
If she sees beyond their hunger
it is censored by instincts
of the nest. A thousand like her live

and perish in the night, their traces
hidden in the grass.

Sundown lights the cholla spines
gold. A breeze sweeps sand against
the ocotillos. High on the cliff,
shadows creep into the redrock
caves.
   Stand here
and turn in every direction...

Requiem

The Authority of Dream said, *take
one final look*, and so, awake,
I run with the fury of grace
down to the wind and water
where the meek green-headed ducks
sail off onto the far fog-shrouded lakes,
where the great blues stilt
in the ink-shadows of calligraphy.

And blown in the tempest of the dream,
I make final pilgrimage to the vast heronries
of heaven, their great nests clotted high
in the dead swamp-drowned cypresses
of the estuaries, the waste-wets,
riverine salt-fields where the tears
of God fall into His old creation crumbling
like glacial till at the horizon
of the up-rolling world. I run west

away from the chaos of the world's
reworking into the wind-blown switchgrass,
into the milfoil fields, low sun in my eyes,
late day colors mixing with indigo
of the failing final night.

I pray for another Ark to come
for this failed-trial world, to salvage
all its intricate work of innocence—
the robed heron, the fire-green duck,

the waving grass, the proud dead tree,
all made to flee the rolling up
of day and night.

For no other world has taken us
like a mother into its meadows
where the sweet strong yeast of love
once dusted down on it until
the heavenly contagion took and spread,
and all things came awake and grew.

From the waiting room window

I watch a crow fly crookedly,
boggled with landing choices. Maybe

this crow thinks too much. The doctor
enters, digresses with pleasantries

before the diagnostic news. Later,
he too will leave, wend his way home,

turn on lights in an empty house.
While the crow and doctor

land, the world gathers
for the next event beyond control.

The crow is out of sight, his receding
caw a black sneer. He says:

This moment slips into the next.
Count on it.

Hawk

To do the most difficult thing, approach
the moment as one who has already died.
—Ruth Benedict (paraphrased)
The Chrysanthemum and the Sword

Keith and I watched Tucker
leave us on the high trail, walk way out
into the shale throat, teetering

stacks of broken rock triggered
for avalanche, at the brink
of oblivion, no blade of green

from there down twenty-two hundred
feet to where a hawk circled
the river gorge below Ontario Peak.

It was a wind-driven day
of brilliant blue. For a long time
Tucker stood there in the mouth

of space, in a communion
we could only watch,
offering himself to the afternoon,

putting a distance between us
we had never known,
between us still.

Bristlecone

Pinus longaeva, the oldest known tree species in the world

Dark particles
from the stars made
carbon-14 from air. The first tree
breathed 14CO2,
time's labeled measurer.

In unknown California
the tree *Promethius* began
in white alkaline dolomite
in the time of Sumer.
Methuselah was traced back
to Giza's pyramids.

> *A strange occurrence of*
> *the simultaneous—Sumer*
> *awakening and these trees,*
> *living monuments of antiquity*
> *that die slowly to live long.*

Twelve more trees were
seedlings in unimaginable
South Park Colorado
when Liu K'un wrote
"A Tartar Maid," and Tao Ch'ien

wrote "Peach Tree Spring"
in the dynasty of Chin.
Another century and more
trees in Colorado's
South Front Range.

Rome began. Buddha woke
into the light under

his tree. Largest of all,
The Patriarch began
in white dolomite where

nothing else will grow—
all this unknown
to Hsiao Kang who wrote
"Dancing Shadows" as
first emperor-poet
of the Liang Dynasty.

Mostly dead wood these
hulks, stunted time travelers
sculpted by flying sand
and ice, *wind timber*
with green pockets linked
by cambium strips down
into the long ago.

Forest

On the John Muir Trail

An odor like a sound
of vast gentleness—

as far as I can see
green dominion of granite
Earth, strung and hovering

to the softest tone. It is
the sound of distance when
there is no sound.

It is the sound of listening
leveled back to white wind,
cold fugues of touch, multitudes

innumerably murmuring, cascading
trebled down ranges
into dawn.

Contact

After *In the Wild: Gray Whales with Christopher Reeve*,
PBS, September 19, 1999

He stands at the launch's bow
grinning and wow-ing
like a ten-year-old at Christmas
as the great gray whale approaches, then
adjusts her huge hull alongside
just close enough for him to reach
and feel her deep softness
in their exchange of curiosity and love.

I thought—here is the moment
the astronomers who search
for intelligent life have waited for. No vigil
beside a dead connection into the night

but here in the blue universe of ocean—
the man, not yet fallen from his horse,
and the vast visitor—
without words to bring back their discovery—
only the applause of waves,
the witness of gulls and winds,
laughing and crying.

Too Late

Dad, the boy who flew home
that night, so full of righteousness,
accusing you—at our last family meal—
of bigotry was not your son,

but some young punk come back
to kick a statue down. But how could I
have known you were vanishing as I lashed out?

Partly out of love I hurt you.
I thought we had time to heal, but forgot
time is only an eternity of goodbyes.
How much of our life was left after that night

and how much bitterness? My apology
came back returned to sender. I'm your age
now, and I carry it with me everywhere.

Genesis

In the beginning was a thing—
somewhere (though "somewhere"
was nowhere).

There was no empty night
with up and down. No space
waiting for stars to light.

A primeval atom, Lemaitre called it
(though atoms have size).
The metaphor—a seed with worlds inside.

But not a seed. A point, a singularity
with dimensions bunched inside,
so tightly wrapped it burst into
the engine of creation.

Then the dimensions unclenched, melted
from ten to four. Collapsing, they sprouted
(the "seed") into a flower of fire.

     If there is God,
     if there was a garden, the Apple,
     Sin, the fall, they must be here
     (in an Eden with no coordinates),
     or nowhere. . .

     Inside the point (no room!)
     the code for apples, fish and caribou,
     and man with his writhing dreams.

If there are souls,
if there is immortality
they are here as well.

We know now we are travelers
flying outward from that first
radio station, static bathing us
in its code of annunciation.

Travellers, we are like the Ouroboros,
the self-swallowing snake, but
in reverse, though, regurgitated from nothingness.
Ex nihilo, Aquinas said.
   (We fly outward, carried
   with astronomers into the stars,
   faster, faster—into endless night)

Perhaps this river path I walk
was once a free quark's leaping track,
fiery dimension ends become
the rainbow in the waterfall.
Thunder of dimensions fusing,
the sound of two wrens answering.

New Poems

Sailing the Bright Stream

into the flow of before and after,
        to enter the current of fathers and mothers,
                you must cast off from certainty,

letting it carry you on into wide waters, following
        the lighted band of a setting sun.
                Later, you will sleep

under an array of summer lights, awakening
        at last to waters without a shore.
                There will be no rehearsal for it

nor anyone to guide you on a journey that you
        will never remember. What began
                as a spring freshet will become your first

Amazon, opening to a shining mirror of sky.
        Beyond the waters, trees on the far bank
                are like dark wishes in their shadows

not of trees left behind, but from ancient hills
        fallen out of sight. Should you look back,
                your point of entry will be gone.

Your memory will not restore any of it
        just as you cannot remember being born.
                Embrace the wonder of that solitude.

Venture on to lost Orinocos of shining water
        where unfamiliar southern stars will look
                down as if in surprise to see you.

Trust curiosity and desire to drive you.
This is the journey imprinted in you by stars
of your nativity. In that solitude

you will never be alone, but among
many warm lights in a regatta, sailing
to lands where waters join the sky.

First Flight Home

After moving east

Flying west over San Gorgonio, *Old Grayback,*
the summit we could never reach on so many hikes,
into the L.A. Basin in deep night,
flaps go down, engines rev, cut back to glide. . .

Below, an endless sea of lights
like the Yuma night sky upside-down,
where we once camped under a brocade
of blazing stars like the cities below us now,
from Banning to Altadena, and all so silent.

The seat-belt lights go on. Down there
every light is someone,
even at the gas stations on Slauson Avenue. Names
of old neighbors, classmates rise from the past.

Everyone I ever knew down there,
winking lights, freeway arteries like shooting stars,
sleepers with their night-lights on.

Looking farther west, I wonder if the lighted fountain
on Wilshire still holds the strange figurine, a little man
with his tiny hands cupping a mystery amid the changing colors?

For several minutes we drift as the lake of lights sweeps out
behind the aircraft, around us in every direction now.
The cabins in Wrightwood are dark, everyone asleep.
Only the black cut-out of Sierra Madres
to the north is pure night on earth.

Below, the senders of light cannot know
how they are alive in my time, alive
in the long past and in a mysterious present,
flying away from us all.

Elixir of Love

From the chorus of "L'Elisir D'Amore"

With the chorus in the wings
I watch tall Nemorino hold
his tiny blue Adina as they sing
of love's Elixir, poured
more than a century ago.

Their voices flare like Bernini's
Glory on Saint Peter's wall,
then soften like the pouring lights
of the *Fontana di Trevi*
in a Roman evening.

How my father loved this music.
Deep in his chair with his glass
and cigar, elegance of Galli-Curci,
Tito Schipa on the old red-seal Victor.

Now, in the curtain shadows,
 he is awake in me—my father,
his tenor ringing *Una furtiva lagrima*,
eyes afire with Donizetti. We join

the man and woman in their music—
in a liturgy older than operas,
old when Tiber's banks were bare,
when Romulus came to the Palatine.

Perennial

Who will I be
waking under a dazzling sky
with strange birds singing
in another century

seeing the ocean
and the green turmoil
of spring
through a child's eyes again?

What will pass between
this moment of light
and that new birth
while I am free

and formless as air?
And when the site where
I am wound and written
is emptied clean

and I am tumbled
from the nest of night
and sight and breathing
thrust on me again

where shall I awake
in that resounding dawn?

Violin

Upon Hearing *Saint-Saëns Violin Concerto, No. 3, Op. 61*

With a voice akin to human.
Its making, a sacrifice to music.

It writes to its love on cream vellum,
crumples the letter and writes

another, with a red wax seal,
a holy command for its preservation.

Under its singing is a story, a cry
that wants to break into words,

a private story in a language
closed in shells of melody.

Its kinship is with needles and branches.
It gives to the wind to set it singing.

It curls into sorrow, then soars
and retreats into warm memory.

It dervishes into freedom then gentles
into cello depths of a waterfall pool.

Its voice is slow fire—flame coded
in lemon, lilac, cobalt, rose, a fountain

of harlequin lights. Ages of elegies tuned
its strings, fresh from its maker's work.

Finally it rises—a yellow Meadowlark!
Its story must be told in peril for its soul.

Star Journey

Sometimes at night I return

to the Griffith Park planetarium

where stars from the surrounding hills

come out to music.

     North of Los Feliz

I step from city lights into the night

sky of Patagonia with its wind-swept shores

under the warm lights of Fornax,

Fomalhaut, Alpha Crucis, a bright canopy

of southern stars, to music—Gymnopedie,

     Satie's *barefoot dance.*

Then, under the soft night sky,

I take off my shoes

and find my way into the stars.

Sailing with Anne

Santa Monica, California, 1950

After her sailing class we cast off
into the ruffled Pacific blue, tide
incoming, echoes of great breakers
lapping the dock. She—the sailor,
the tiller, mine.

As we headed west, tacking
into a strong breeze I remember
marveling at who she was
to do these things. I imagined her
at the helm become Anne Bonny,
running a four-master down,
the setting sun turning red lights
in her hair.

I hope we left something there—
if only a boat paint-scrape
or salt spray from her hair.
Maybe something from that day
was never lost, but joined
the Pacific's history, some trace
still riding the blue circuit
between the poles, with the sea-grape
and tiny life that make the coral.

Thin Air

Just past Wilson's Cienega
hiking the San Jacinto trail
a Haiku came down
from the blue ozone sky
so I wrote it out in my mind
scrambling around rock slides
through scrub pines and oak
just over ten thousand feet
as I looked down
to where I once got lost
a whole day in sunlit Long Valley
then far into the gray forever
the poem safe inside.
I kept on through Manzanita,
blackjack oak, chinquapin,
wild springs bubbling up
everywhere, sun hot in the thin air
past dark granite walls
with sparkling mica changing
sun colors in the high blue.
Up at the summit
there was a tin can
with a tiny spiral booklet,
a pencil tied to it
previously signed by "Sky-High Joe"
        who said (in 1994)
You must be drunk or stupid to be here.
Joe left a space below for my Haiku, but
it was gone, every word gone
somewhere back down the trail
waiting for some lucky poet to find.

Tennessee Night Fire

A ghost in gossamer orange,
it's a wild hunger that wants to leap
its pit and eat this dry field.
Two guitar men scoot back from the heat.
They try to ignite the crowd into a song. . .

O my loving brother, when the world's on fire,
Don't you want God's bosom to be your pillow?
O carry me over to the rock of ages,
Rock of ages, cleft for me.

Nestor, a young Columbian, plays
a song of Medellin. I catch some Spanish:
"Si, campo is field," he says. He wants to open
a café in America and cook *Fritanga*, where

"it is less dangerous than home."
Nestor hands his guitar to Jimmy, just back
from Montreal. Jimmy tries out some

Quebecois French, tells Nestor about
great tour guide wages in Canada.
So earnest, so fragile these boys,
they connect like gravity.

Over the vast surround of hills
their dreams flower into the night
as they audition before the nothingness
that goes on and on.

Eyes Open Prayer

O you without name
always arriving
in the dark above me,
guest needing no

invitation, fusion
of all loves I have known
from childhood,
you who comes as a wild

fragrance with bright
surprises, remnant
of those passed
from daylight

I can no longer reach.
Extravagant font
of patience
from a love I did not

recognize, I know you
will be with me,
the final light
of my last gathering

when life
flows into time.

The Dance

I say yes to the tulip tree
dropping its cups of flowers,
golden and green
          and to the derelict ailanthus
          breaker of concrete sidewalks
and to the sumac with its cones of fire.

Yes to the white-tails that float
their magic, then vanish
far into the woods' deep green
          and to the mallard pair, duck and drake
          that waddle up from Crabtree Creek
and to the earthworms
they clear from our driveway.

Yes to the turtle, the red slider
that spring calls from the creek
to wandering, the one I rescued
from a storm-drain and gave my blessing to.
          And yes to that damn beaver
          that cut down the giant beech
near the stream, my favorite tree
in the wetland, and to the trees
he left behind.

Yes to the night's extravagance of stars,
to Vega's frozen light, the lyre of the stars
and to the southern cross
and multitudes of strange lights
I cannot see, much less name, so far below

the horizon over Patagonia
all the way down to the pole.

And yes to the blessing of day and night,
mates following each other
and to the contentment each brings
in its own way, bright, then silent dark.

Because none of these I can keep.
They are not mine, and I cannot stop
the music in the middle of the dance.

So yes to this morning rain carrying
yesterday away.

David Treadway Manning is a Pushcart nominee and three-time winner of the North Carolina Poetry Society's Poet Laureate Award. His poems have appeared in *Southern Poetry Review*, *Tar River Poetry*, *Rattle*, *32 Poems*, and also *Literary Trails of Eastern North Carolina: A Guidebook*, edited by Geogann Eubanks (UNC Press). He is a past winner of the Longleaf Chapbook competition and of Crucible's Sam Ragan Award. He has ten chapbooks, most recently *Singularities* (Finishing Line Press, 2018). His full-length works include *The Flower Sermon*, runner-up for the 2007 Main Street Rag Poetry Book Award: *Soledad* (Main Street Rag, 2014); and the unserious Yodeling Fungus (Old Mountain Press. 2010). As the convenor of the Friday Noon Poets of Chapel Hill, he was coeditor of the group's anthology, *Always on Friday* (Katherine James Books, 2006). David and his wife Doris live in Cary, North Carolina.

Photo: David, about age eleven, with his beloved desert tortoises.